The Sky Was Empty, but Still the Thunder Rolled

The Sky Was Empty, but Still the Thunder Rolled

DOMINIC LYNE

QUEERMOJO
A Rebel Satori Imprint

New Orleans & New York

Published in the United States of America by
REBEL SATORI PRESS
rebelsatori.com

ISBN: 978-1-60864-347-9

Cover Image by Dominic Lyne
Book Design by Sven Davisson

For Tree.

Things you said still saved in my iPhone Notes:
"Death Baby fucks the Corn God."
"He did so many drugs it gave him brain damage."
"Boat."

Act One:
The Raven and the Wolf

one

It generally starts with a photo,
our social life god Facebook,
in its omnipresent wisdom,
draws my attention
towards the memories of mine
it stores digitally.
Their 1s and 0s
slip through
the pinprick cracks around my safe
and force it open
before dispersing on a waveform,
leaving the true physical memory
exposed and naked.
Just writing
the last three words of that sentence
creates a sense of foreboding.
I know where this is going.
I know how it ends.

We were at a house party,
I cannot remember where.
Her and I,
a group of others,
most of whom I did not know,
a few by faces only.
That did not matter,
it could have been just her and I,
surrounded by our own bubble,
high, drinking fruit juice.
No alcohol.
We did not drink alcohol,
but drugs were fine.
Noses powdered with MDMA and cocaine,

the rough and the dignified.
A perfect analogy of us.
My roughness mixed with her elegance
created a drug so perfect that
not even heroin could have a chance
of winning my affection.
And why would it?
Brown rotted my soul,
she made it sing.

My T-shirt said "dope" on it,
a cross separating each letter,
an anchor printed
at the bottom, just above my groin.
That T-shirt summed up
the days leading to this moment:
strung out on heroin,
I had dropped my anchor into
the unseen lake that exists beyond
the cave entrance of an anus.
I had fucked some random guy
on the bed of a thirteen year old.
It was not as sordid as you have
allowed your mind to sink.
It was the son's of another friend –
the bed, not the anus –
who was not home.
For clarity, the guy was eighteen.
I had just turned thirty.
I added that for ego purposes.
This is not relevant, I am deflecting;
trying to bury one memory
with the rubble of another.

The original is not actually a bad one.
It is just a keyframe

too close to the end of a movie
you wish would go on forever.
Enjoy these lighthearted moments,
they disappear pretty quick.

Jaws sore from laughter,
nonstop and uncontrolled.
Separated from reality by the "tee-hees",
our minds broadcasting television
produced by LSD.
The chair devoured us,
it broke us down like a Venus Flytrap;
spitting out the remains across the floor.

"I love you," Tree said,
pulling herself free from
chlorophylled digestive fluids.
I bent double, trying to breathe,
watching her pick herself up.
"I love you, Dom."
"You already said that."
"Well, you doubly know now, don't you."

*   *   *

The night bus' engine fell quiet.
Lost in our own world
we had not seen the bus empty around us.
"What's that fucking noise?" I moaned.
The constant distorted looped mumble
was attempting to push its thumb
down on my high;
hoping, it seemed, to crush it
like a sociopathic child does an ant
in a precursor to a future
diagnosis of antisocial personality disorder.

The same psychopathic tendencies as the driver
who, approaching us angrily,
shouted for us to get off the bus.
Stumbling towards the exit,
I finally process the tinny mumble and note
it is the voice of Siri's older sister.
"This bus terminates here."
Fuck you.

Standing on the pavement,
surrounded by unfamiliar scenery,
an abscess of apprehension threatens to pop;
to evacuate a torrent of pus-leaden panic.
Stay focused, Dom,
it is just a micro-diversion.
"Where the fuck are we, Tree?"
The answer was instant.
"We are here."
"But where is 'here' exactly?"
"Here."

two

[*Rustle, rustle*]
"I hate my phone."
[*Click*]
"End of message.
To listen to this message again, please press 1;
to delete, press 2."
[*Beep*]

[*Rustle, rustle*]
"I hate my phone."
[*Click*]
"End of message.
To listen to this message again, please press 1;
to delete, press 2."
[*Beep*]

[*Rustle, rustle*]
"I hate my phone."
[*Click*]
"End of message.
To listen to this message again, please—

Her voice.
What is this little sentence?
The voice of a ghost?
No, it cannot be a ghost,
the voice of a ghost is captured after death,
faint whispers
hidden beneath layers of static and noise.
This was captured in life;
her voice converted to 1s and 0s,
on replay reverted back to physical waves,
A portion of her essence remains alive,

tangible.
It is all I have left.
Not connected to any visuals
that trap her as a memory,
she could have left this today,
yesterday,
tomorrow.
The words will never change.

Who am I kidding?
Simply a stone-tape recording.
The past looped.
When she left, the sound quality changed.
It became empty.
Hollow.
It sounds like what my voice became too.

three

As the date gets closer,
my mind begins to shadow.
Storm clouds form and soon
they will cover the sky.
Shades of grey, maybe flecks of white
representing those tiny moments
when something tricks my brain
into thinking about something else.
Minuscule dots of no colour,
but no gaps revealing the sky;
no warmth from the hidden sun.
Clouds so deep and ominous
their weight is transferred to my spine,
pushed closer towards Hell in a stoop that says:
*This sadness should not belong
in someone so young.*

I am not young however,
this soul is old, ancient.
A spiritual life cord
weaved so tightly into the fabric of time
that should the thread snap,
a fresh start could be made and
the quilt of eternity would not unravel.
For all extents and purposes
the backbone would remain as though intact,
the cursed legacy remaining unbroken.

Look at those clouds,
filled with so much water that
should they burst, the world
would be drowned in grief
tenfold.

Noah's flood would be reduced to a mere footnote;
the mountains of Ararat as lost to humanity
as the Garden of Eden.
But they will not break, I will not allow them.
Mankind deserves to burn
with fire and brimstone,
its skin turned molten,
blood evaporated into the atmosphere
where it can condense and rain down upon
its own charred remains.
Drowning for a second time
would be too easy a conclusion.

The purest angel passed and
they turned it into a spectacle for their amusement.
A monument of amethyst should have been erected,
instead they built a Big Top.
I stood at its centre,
my feet covered in sawdust,
exposed by the spotlight as though I was the main act.
They all sat in their seats,
popcorn and candy
filling their mouths in a metachronal wave;
an undulating, unbroken circle
that prevented my exit.
They waited for me to crack, waited
for the first sight of a glistening line from my eye
down to the shit encrusted floor.

You waited
but it never came. I denied you.
You have never let me forget.
I was not the main attraction,
that was enacted just to my right.
You denied it of its witness.
Karma will never let you forget.

That date is approaching,
their singular annual posts on her wall,
reminded to them by a faceless Facebook,
does nothing to ease their guilt.
You cannot think of her without thinking of me;
I will always be stood next to her,
both of us blurred like ghosts,
together watching you burn in Hell.

four

Breathe.
Slow, deep breaths.
Let the oxygen,
filtered through cancer,
fill my lungs and hold;
as if letting it sit there
will have some beneficial
affect on my emotions.
Wishful thinking.
There is no pill that could achieve that.
The only thing that comes close is
a brown powder
that goes on to define me.
So much easier to call someone a junkie,
a weak willed soul
locked in a relationship of chasing the dragon.
Never mind the reason for it.
Never mind the obvious cry for help.
Just point the finger and laugh,
roll your eyes, hell,
why not blame him for your own unhappiness.

Imagine a pain so great
that the only way to continue
is to numb it chemically.
The pain was not physical but it agonised
more than anything I had ever experienced
through thirty years of living.

Fuck it.
Ten minutes have passed.
Staring into nothing.
Even now

I do not know how to express it—
Fuck this,
I cannot do this tonight.

The second I put the lid on my pen,
all noise disappears and
my searching mind is sucked into a vacuum
to float around in space without a paddle.
Each star may contain an answer I seek,
only I will be the dust of dust
before I am even a tenth of the way towards it.
It will just burn itself out
with the powerful knowledge it knows.
Itself long dead before anyone
notices its disappearance.

Thankfully I stare into space
and not a mirror.

five

Tonight the northern lights
flicked digitally across the London sky.
Pixelated light
through machine spewed fog.
As pretty as it was
it had a tinge of deceit,
something off, like a memory,
always rerun with a glossy sheen.
Veneers glued over rotting teeth.

The photographs display happiness.
That much was true.
The first time everyone in the room
accepted each other,
what I had waited for across different lifetimes.
The past merged with the present
giving hope for the future that never came.
The paint over mould stains.
Scratch beneath the surface,
it does not take much to dislodge the truth.
I was the darkness in the light.
The cum-stain on the Pope's bedsheets.

Deep in addiction,
pipe tucked between my ass and balls,
taking quick trips to the bathroom
to breathe in the dragon's tail.
She knew, she had always known.
The only one I told, the only one
who did not change how they saw me.
Beautiful like that.
Looked past everything to see the soul beneath.
"You complete me," she said on many occasions.

Instead of flinching away from my darkness,
she found the break in her light
where she could fit it in
like a missing piece of a jigsaw puzzle,
allowing it to become part of her.

All my life I have felt incomplete,
something missing, but since meeting you
that feeling has gone. I feel complete.
You are the darkness to my light.
I feel whole for the first time in my life.

Hold a mirror up to those words,
they could have come from my lips.
My mouth could have formed the mirrored image
from the other side of the glass.
We all know it is darker in the reflected world.
Two halves connected
with such an explosion that reality could not cope.
Mother Nature pissed that
winter fell in love with summer.
What is completed gets broken much easier.
I am glad her last moments would be
played in the context of being whole,
but for me the cracks hurt more than ever before.
For a moment, a brief wish
that I had never experienced peace,
as watching it crumble to dust—
You cannot miss what you never had.
I had it, and I have never missed
anything as much as this.

That veneer again. If only we knew
our time was running out on that day.
Exactly one month left.
Four weeks.

Such precious little seconds
counting down in ignorance.
From the depths of rock bottom,
I had clawed my way back to the brim of contentment,
my eyes cast to the future.
My future. Our future.
Little did I know.

My saviour's wings were wrapped tightly around me,
and in their warmth I found peace.

SIX

Time was slipping away.
Who knew that memories would soon become tributes?
Memories would be all I have,
frozen in time, no new ones made.
Bookended between
first meeting and death.

You chose to pursue my friendship,
to force yourself into my life.
I opened myself to you.
Fate forced you out.
If you knew this would be the conclusion,
would you have even bothered?

seven

A flash of purple captures my eye
wherever I go, and in that moment
I know that you are there,
watching over me,
reminding me
that you have not abandoned this damaged creature
as he continues to wander through life.
Leaving markers to show that I am not stumbling aimlessly
but am exactly where I am meant to be at any given moment.
You always said everything happens for a reason,
even if that is not clear from the outset;
and fuck me, many of the reasons for my existence
continue to hide themselves in the shadows,
held firmly in the grip of the darkness
that not even my jailer, the shadow man, knows.
My life is a mystery that you tried to help me unpick the lock
that would allow confusion to become acceptance and
    understanding.
We managed to peep through the keyhole,
saw only more pinpricks of light that suggested
a galaxy of other keyholes.
It may have seemed like a needle in a haystack,
but it told us that there were many doors available to me.

So many doors, so many choices,
so many outcomes, but none could give me what I truly desire.
None could bring you back to me.
None could shine as bright as I wish.
Everything is tainted by your absence.
How could someone who forced themselves into my life
for such a small portion of it
leave such a mark that nothing would ever feel complete
in their absence?

I guess that is another one of those unexplained reasons.

I do not believe that the darkness planned for you to burst through
its tightly scheduled plot of my life's story.
You were not placed in my path for me to meet,
or to fulfil a designated role.
You were an extra on the set of a singular scene who wanted more
and made sure you got it.
I am so glad that you did.
The rebel who defied the scriptwriter, director and producer.
That was the type of person you were.
I would have loved to see the looks on their faces.
Maybe one day I will.

Even now with your purple breadcrumbs, you defy them.
The darkness took you away from me,
but when did anything it did prevent you from placing
your hand upon mine?

You are the dawn that breaks the darkness.

eight

How would you like me to remember you?
Not in sadness, but with love.
An alabaster bust carved to perfection,
placed upon a pedestal for all to see.
In snow white purity you could gaze
forever at the world that fascinated you
in never-ending ways.
Always finding a beauty in anyone,
even when it was hidden so deep beneath the surface.
A more forgiving being than even God Himself.
His eyes never quested through the circles of Hell
to gaze upon Lucifer's beautiful face
in search for even a glimmer of remorse.

I have not turned you into a baseless idol in your absence.
I remember you just as I did
when you sat perched on the battered sofa.
From my corner on the floor,
even the decrepitude of my sanctuary
could not make you appear any less selfless than you were.
You were not perfect, but to me you were
a perfect example that there existed some hope
that humanity could be found in one place,
not spread throughout multiple faces
of people with multiple faces.

How should I remember you?
As my soulmate, the Yang to my Yin.
Tàiyīn and *Tàiyáng*.
Place half of my moon next to half of your sun
to create the never-ending circle of life.

A memory.

Me stumbling down the stairs of a club, you walking up them.
Baggy in hand I ask you to cover me
as I stick a note in and inhale energy into my body.
I turn to say "thank you",
but find your finger in my mouth,
rubbing MDMA into my gums.
What better image of decadence could I have asked for?

You scarred my soul,
my beloved magpie.
We were two for joy.
I am one for sorrow.

That is how I will remember you, my dearest Tree.
Tears of happiness.
Smiles of despair.

nine

"Please don't leave without saying 'goodbye'.
Promise me that, Dom."
"I promise."

You left without saying "Goodbye."

ten

You can try to bury your sadness,
yet no matter how deep you hide it,
your eyes will forever betray you.
Each time you stare into a mirror,
they show it reflected back at you.
Eye to eye.
No escape.
Better to embrace it
than let it eat away from within.

eleven

I was about to admit that I am not spiritual,
but that would be a lie.
It was one of the many things that pulled us together,
allowing many conversations to bubble to the surface
and break upon shared thoughts.

You never wanted to 'solve' me,
so respectful of a shadow neither of us understood.
It held you in the palm of its hand one day,
caged your soul to the soundtrack of my voice.
Cold, oppressive.
Something happened in that moment that sowed the seeds
of what would come.

Shall I wait and carefully word the wishes I should make
to the New Moon on the fifth.
Could they bend reality and allow the impossible
to remove its negative?
Could they, if I squeezed my eyes tight enough,
force my vision to transcend between realms,
summon into existence an image of you,
crisp and clear in ultra high definition that
I could hear the "tee-hee" of your laugh
just by the way my memory animates your form.
If I wished hard enough could I coax out one final
"I love you,"
from your digital lips?

You exist as binary code. 1s and 0s.
Quite fitting given that there was once
one of you,
and now there is
zero.

twelve

"Imagine the person who you would most like to see,"
the woman stood in front of the pews says,
the altar behind her;
behind that the stained glass window depicting
Christ risen from the dead.
"Now imagine turning and seeing them
stood at the back of this church.
What would you do?"

I would run,
forget the formalities of the service at hand.
I would run and embrace you.
I would not question what I saw.
Delusion or Divine act, I would not care;
I could be stood hugging nothing but cold air,
it would matter not,
for those moments would be the realisation of
the one single desire I have.

Yet, you are not Christ.
No matter how many songs I raise up in praise
they all fall short and God fails to notice,
crushing them beneath His feet as He walks
through the dew coated grass.
You were not born from His loins
so why would He so much as blink in your direction.
You will not rise from the grave,
you will not be standing behind me in this dusty cold church.
You will never be at my side again,
but you are always by my side.

Who cares if God decides to reanimate you or not?
When have I ever cared about what He wills?

I would bring you back in a heartbeat.
I'm going to say it:
"Fuck Christ, I didn't know Him.
Give me someone I care about."

I shouted at Christ for you,
who else could say that?
Who else stood before Him and
demanded an answer, a reason?
Who else?
Yet I will always be the perpetual villain.
Who would want a saviour like me,
when they have experienced one like you?

I do not need to look behind me
because that was a position you never stood in.
Behind me is only dust.
Dust represents history.
History means past.
Past means end.
Gone.
Happened.
Finished.
Those are words that sound cheap
when laid at your feet.
If God can walk on the crushed dreams of millions,
you can walk on the dreams of trillions.

thirteen

You stood up for me when no one else did.
Fought my corner even though it made
your so called friends distance themselves from you.
I say 'so called' because
their dislike of me was greater than their love of you.
That I cannot understand.
I had done nothing to warrant that hatred,
they all knew it was based on a lie,
yet that lie was of more importance to their fragile egos
than any truth you tried to suggest.

You did not miss them you said,
but I could see in your eyes that it hurt;
again I could not understand why you chose
to experience such pain
rather than just nod and prolong their lies.
The moment you made that choice
I can picture as though it was yesterday.
You took my hand and took a side.
Squeezing gently, you told me truths
I already knew, had already worked out.
You told me nothing new,
yet the revelation was ground breaking.
Seismic. Atomic.
A Hiroshima of friendship.
This I had never experienced,
it felt amazing.
Who would throw that away for a lie?
They did.

They threw you away and as a result
missed the ending.
Their final memories ones of deceit.

So in your absence they told more lies,
which they would convince themselves
were true.
I was the villain who stole you away,
who polluted your mind against them.
They were your 'brothers' and 'sisters'
pushed away by the untrustworthy black sheep.
If you had chosen their lies
you would still be alive,
because the truth kills.

Your friendship to me was cancer,
it ate you up, rotted you from the inside out.
They were not happy you met me,
even though it was them who pushed us
closer together.
The sinners will always play the victim,
hide the truth in the same place they hide their guilt.
The real victim is made the scapegoat.
As they cut me down,
spilling my blood across the soil
as a sacrifice to their God of Lies,
I whisper a promise to you.
My weeds will always strangle their corn.

fourteen

We spent the day laughing,
set off by anything;
ghosts of reasons left behind
in tears of happiness
that rained down and
turned dust into the mud of memory.
Conversations forgotten,
words spoken without thought;
a commodity.

In their abundance they are
thrown around like spring flowers,
pretty but replaceable.

In their absence,
the winter sets root,
existing in a barren landscape,
cold, empty,
dead.

fifteen

It remains a crime
that this existence of mine continues
whilst yours does not.
Sat in the sun that will never touch your face,
I remember you sat next to me,
holding my hand as you cried
for the pain I have lived through;
who is here to hold my hand
against the pain of your absence?
I imagine you next to me,
reaching with your hand,
trying to touch mine;
both of us crying for the other,
both wanting to feel the same sun
dry our eyes.
I wish my imagination was truth,
but they would only raise my medication
to pull you further away from me.
In this pain I am alone.
No amount of wishing could bring you back,
knowing this I continue to wish everyday.
Insanity, is, after all, doing the same thing
again and again,
expecting a different result.

A blurred photograph.
Life seen through a cracked lens.
Broken.
Imperfect.
Incomplete.
Memories fade, like polaroids.
Shadows of their former selves.
Only one remains picture perfect.

Relived at a moments notice.
Transported back.
A stranger who failed to save your life
puts her hand on my shoulder.
"You did everything you could.
She would have been proud."
Failure comforting failure,
remains failure.

sixteen

Same church where I shouted at God, Christ, whoever.
A year later I cried at an altar to a God I once believed in.
On my knees, donation paid to light a candle in your honour.
Typical Catholic Church, prayers will only reach Heaven
if covered in gold.
I would rather pay the ferryman, but hey, what are you to do?
Maybe you will hear it, maybe not.

I have never cried in a church outside of a funeral,
maybe these were the tears I held back at yours.
Brave face against the glares of all those who probably thought
I had no right to be there.
At least now they have been cried, just another layer of grief shed,
but never enough to peel back to the core.
I will grieve for a thousand lifetimes
for what was stolen from this one.

I should not be lighting candles for your memory.
I should be lighting the end of your *Vogue* cigarettes
as we dance the night away with careless abandon.
Now I do not even want to dance.
Nothing hurts more than the morning after
when you are not sat opposite me,
both of us looking like shit to everyone else,
but perfect to each other.

Once you have had perfection,
everything else seems so pale.

seventeen

Wake up to that sound,
that final sound that rattled out of your mouth
as you fell away from me.
The sound my mother would tell me was
the sound of you dying;
the end of all hope,
everything that followed just
a prerequisite for the grave.

How could that ugly sound
be the last of your beautiful life
exiting this world?
To be honest, I did not need to be told.
I could tell in your eyes,
as all life drained from them,
reflecting only my panicked face,
my scream down the phone.
A woman in an anonymous call-centre
the only witness to the sounds
of your demise.

I hate that word: *demise.*
It brings to mind the end of empires
crumbling under the weight of their own decadence.
It was not your demise heard, it was mine.
My empire crushed by its own weight.
What was it my father said?
There was no surprise.
How else does a junkie think his world would end?
With lilies sprouting from the tips of needles
used to push life into veins so devoid of happiness,
so vacant and empty that all goodness gets burnt on a pipe
made from a bottle from which he never drank.

No, your life ended that day; mine demised.
Its walls became putrid barriers
sealing in rat infested plagues.
You escaped my pestilence,
you escaped my gutter,
creating a star in the sky too high to reach,
but to what I will always stare up to.

Junkies never receive riches,
the only gold we hold is the golden brown
that tattoos our pathetic existence
through lives with more pain than joy.
I actually believed what you said,
who would not?
I still know it was not a lie,
but you did tell me one.
You promised you would be with me,
that every step I took would be shadowed by yours.
The truth is they are shadowed by Death,
my only constant companion.
You promised to say "Goodbye."

You never said "Goodbye."
This I can forgive,
Death took you before you realised.
Those final thoughts you worded
were just thoughts,
spoken between you and I.
Something precious, yet so sad.
We laughed after you said them.
Who knew.
Who knew.
I wish I did.
I would have savoured them
even though it would have been
the bite of the apple that locked shut
the Gates of Eden.

32

eighteen

There comes a point when words are not enough,
could never be enough.
How many times can you attempt to write the unwritable
and expect it to be enough?
I was not good enough to save your life,
how could I be good enough to write about your death?

I can see that moment so clearly, so vividly.
I can get lost in it so completely each time I try
to rewrite the outcome;
failing and watching everything act out exactly the same.
You cannot change the past,
no matter how much you try.
The final image is always the same.
Everything I want, everyone I need lies broken,
dead in front of me.

Dead.

Dead.

Death lies before me.
You made the exit I long to make;
the exit you talked me away from.
You left and did not take me with you.
You left me alone.
An hour previous we had been two.
Then we became one.

Five times I walked past you.
Five times I tried to not look at you.
Five times my heart re-broke as I failed,
wanting you to just sit up.

One big, sick joke.
Five times I knew that would never happen.
Five.
Two plus three.
Twenty-Three.
That number.
Of course that number would be present.
The number that stalks me,
the number of the shadow,
of the darkness.
Twenty-fucking-three.
Five times.

Numerology number five.
Someone who is full of energy,
unable to channel it responsibly.
How like us.
Your energy;
my inability to channel mine responsibly.
Channelling it through lines of powder,
chasing it though homemade pipes.
As your soul sails down the five rivers
in the realm of Hades,
the water from the underworld
streams down my face from eyes imprinted
with the image of your mortal form,
lying in its final position,
staring up at a ceiling you could not see.

Then the part no one knows,
no one cared to ask or bothered to understand.
It had been only us,
everything witnessed only by two pairs of eyes,
one now blind, the other a suspect
to a sudden unexpected death.
Suspect.

A finger of blame uncurling in my direction.
A death in the house of a junkie.
Suspicion.
Had the drugs been taken willingly?
Had I slipped you some heroin?
"It is just a formality," they said.
It hit like an accusation,
hung in the air like the scent of—

Led away in a police car and questioned.
I seemed to know so little about a body
I 'claimed' to belong to my best friend.
I did not just lose my friend, my soul mate,
I was caught with heroin.
Questioned like a stranger.
The mysterious junkie,
that was the line taken by everyone,
taken and ran with.
"You are just a junkie."
"Nobody here has a good word to say about you."
"She was fine before she met you."
Slap after slap across a face
that was not allowed to grieve.
A face that turned to stone out of spite.
Liars would not see me break,
their lies would not break me.

My time to grieve was stolen from me.
Everything was stolen from me.
I lost everything;
lost everyone in such a short space of time.
Dominos of pain clattering against each other,
racing towards oblivion.
A black line of despair
that ended in a pile of brown.
Numbed, played into a reputation.

Rock bottom, all your feet on my back.
Keeping me there,
keeping me where you wanted and
happily I obliged.
Dirt is all I am,
dirt is all I wanted.
I played your junkie scapegoat,
you played the funeral entourage.

Your truth is hollow and vacant,
like your souls, like your futures.
She is waiting for me.
She is by my side.
She is with me.
She chose to be my shadow.
I bet that burns like acid,
but that is the grave you all made.
Go lie in it.
I know truths that could ease your pain,
they will die with me, unspoken, untold.
You all chose to let me burn,
I chose indifference to you all.
You are not worth my anger.
You are not worth my time.
I have spoken my last about you.

nineteen

"Are you not doing your make-up?"
"I don't wear make-up."
That was our first conversation.
Awkward. Passing.
Nothing about it stood out.
I walked away and that was that.
Not for you.
I do not know what you saw, felt;
something about my aloof,
cold countenance captivated you.
A chance meeting set in motion
something so beautiful and unexpected.

I have asked myself so many times
what it could have been.
Stared at my reflection,
searched the visible
for a reason not physical.
It was not something you saw,
it was something you did not.
I was a puzzle with a missing piece,
frustratingly incomplete.
Most had abandoned the search
for what was lost. Not you.
You wanted to solve the unsolvable,
even if the unsolvable did not want to be solved.
You went out of your way
to be a part of my life
with such passion that there was no way
I could escape.
We laughed about it many times.
Even you did not know what compelled you
to be so focused on that single goal.

I intrigued you, other than that it was
just a desire to be my friend.
I think it was because, unbeknownst to us,
you were the missing piece,
that is why we clicked together so perfectly.

For a moment we were complete,
for the first time in both our lives.
We both felt it, we both knew it,
so when you left,
you did not take away the original piece,
you took a new piece;
with that I felt the incompleteness afresh.
Brand new. Alien.
I have lived my life feeling incomplete,
I was comfortable with that.
Now I am lost and incomplete,
uncomfortable.
You completed me,
you destroyed me.
I am a ruin of a ruin;
I know that because of this,
you are a ruin too.
I wish you were smiling right now;
I know that you are crying.

I want to cry right now,
cry out in frustration
that I cannot word what I feel,
running off in tangents that focus
on anyone else but you.
Shooting bullets is easy
when your gun is pointed at those
who have done you wrong.
Pull the trigger and leave ink spills across a page,
stepping over their narrative corpse,

walking away satisfied.
I do not want to write about them anymore,
I want to stay focused on you.
Anger and pain always pull attention
away from what is important.
If it was not for them,
I would not have met you,
so for that I should be thankful,
and I am,
but their service is now complete.
They have been tipped,
who remembers the busboys at a hotel?

Bang! Bang!

twenty

I have seen death,
I have seen it make its visit and then depart.
Death so cowardly that it hides itself from sight.
Its actions witnessable, itself witnessless.
That is the way it has to be.
If Death could be seen, it could be fought.
Could you kill Death?
Lucky for it I could not witness it
pulling you away from me,
I would have let go of your hand,
taken both of mine and choked
the life out of Death.
It would have been Death's eyes that dulled,
not yours.
It would have been Death's body sprawled
on the carpeted floor.
As Death lay there I would have returned to you.
No ambulance would have been called.
No paramedics would have crowded around it.
I would not have allowed any access to anyone
who could try to resuscitate Death.
I would have let Death die
for trying to take you away.
I would have taken Death's corpse,
thrown it in the canal,
its cowl weighted with bricks.
I would have watched Death sink.
I would let it disappear.
I would be the only witness.

That is what I would have done if I could see Death,
however, I can't.
So instead I watched it pull you away.

I watched paramedics take over from me.
I watched as one approached and told me
they had ceased their efforts.
I watched the future crumble.
I watched you leave.
I watched Death without seeing it.

What have my eyes seen?
They have seen happiness crushed
time and time again.
They have seen so much pain,
so much loneliness,
so much disappointment.
No matter how many volumes
of positive experiences stand
cover-to-cover on the shelf,
they are always bookended with negativity.

twenty-one

It is always the same.
The long walk of dread as I approach.
The reality of it confirmed when
from across the sea of headstones
I see your face staring out of black marble.
A deep sinking feeling bringing to the fore
the infinite hole at my core,
as it rushes forward to make connection to
the final resting place of your physical existence.
In its aim it connects, as I sit next to you,
the emptiness feels full.
Even in death you complete me.

I could sit here for the rest of my waking life.
Ageing alongside your permanent beauty.
Never alone.
The place of my greatest sorrow,
the only place I feel completely at peace.
Although I feel you with me,
the silence reminds me that you are not.
No one could talk more than you,
not even myself.

I would give everything for
one more conversation.
It would be all I needed to continue
with the nothing I would be left with.
To hear your voice once again
say something new,
that I could record and loop continuously,
knowing how important it is,
unlike all those carefree words we let
ourselves forget.

Today the same sun warms us together,
I can share these words with you and
know that you hear them.
Sharing tears across domains.
Tears on Earth, tears in Heaven.
Once we were connected by happiness,
now we are connected by sadness.
As I write those last words,
clouds blocked out the sun,
that brief moment of cold darkness
your confirmation;
the sun's warm return proving
this is not how it will end.
We will be reunited again someday,
this phase of despair will be
a tiny black mark on the page of our friendship.
Not a full stop, but a semi-colon.
A longer breath than a comma,
but one that has a future still to be written.

Maybe this was why you never said "Goodbye."
You knew that it was not the end,
it was just a pause in our joint existence
as we set out on journeys we needed
to experience alone.
You gave me the tools and faith
I needed for this solitary path.
You gave me the energy and mindset
to be able to survive this journey
from the darkness to the light.
You gave me the torch to light the way
through the inky blackness.
You gave me the will to go on living.
You pulled me from the pits of self-loathing,
of no hope.
You did this so selflessly.

You set me back on my feet.
You gave me something I had never truly had.
You believed in me. One hundred percent.
You gave me hope for the future.
I am alive because of you,
because of that I was there to comfort you
in the final moments of your story.
We did not write the ending,
just the prelude to the next chapter.

I am alive because of you.
I will keep you alive in my heart.

twenty-two

Leaving is always the hardest.
Rising to my feet, I often return to the ground.
Just another minute, five, ten, thirty.
I could stay forever, but unfortunately for me life continues.
Other responsibilities pull me away,
and as my heart tries to heavy itself into an anchor,
I kiss your cold forehead and turn away.
I say "Goodbye" each and every time. We learnt the hard way
that precious things can be stolen away in a heartbeat.

Each exit feels like I am losing you again.
The chasm within empties with each step I take away.
What had temporarily filled is emptied,
the hole of your absence returns to its black void,
consuming any happiness around it;
leaving every positive experience
with a postscript beginning with *but*.

You left such a big mark on my life that in your absence
everything feels lacking. A life that existed completely before you
now never feels complete. That says so much to me, and in
those moments of wished attendance I remember that I actually
know your reaction, the words you would say:
"That was amazing, Dom."
"You are amazing, Dom."
I picture the smile those words would be coupled with, the hug,
the hand squeeze... the hand squeeze.

Flashback.
Your hand goes limp in mine, your eyes lose their light,
you are falling away from me, my life falls apart.
"I am going to guide you through it.
Check her airways are not blocked.

45

Tilt her head back and breathe into her mouth."
My last kiss, the kiss of life, a kiss of death.

I pause, close my eyes to the replay.
I open them. "Is that an important phone call?"
"No."
"Can you please end it." I ended it.
"We are going to discontinue with the CPR.
She was unresponsive."
You were dead, the news of that crushed me.
The weight so heavy that it broke my spine. Paralysed, but
who needs to walk when there is no journey to be made?
Your postscript began in that moment.

"But you must go on."
I can see your face filled with determination,
the face that would not accept the word *no*.
"I will not be the reason you do not succeed.
I will not be the boulder that blocks the road.
I will not be the excuse for you to give up."
You are not any of those.
You are my inspiration,
I will dedicate libraries worth of books to your memory.
I will not let you be the reason I give up,
nor the excuse to put down my pen.

You let the shadow hold you in his palm
just so you could listen to my words.
That bravery and belief in me and what I transcribe
is something I can never ignore.
You let the darkness touch your soul
to hear my writing read aloud,
my dearest Tree, my most beautiful friend,
you were, are, will always be an angel to me.

twenty-three

I sensed you near me the other day.
A wave of calm breathed over me,
silencing the voices in my head,
as watching videos from the happiest day in my life
brought my mind back to the story's bitter end.
We were just laughing,
I cannot remember what set us all off,
I remember the pleasant ache in my jaw and chest
from laughing too hard.

Commence et la fin.
The beginning and the end.
La fin trop tôt.
Le début trop tard.

If only I had not resisted your initial attempts
at getting close, put aside my stupid issues of trust,
and just let you in.
Pulled open the door and opened my arms.
There would have been more memories created
that I could tell, instead of boring everyone with
the only collection I have.

Everyone gave us space, sat away from us,
unable to break their way into the bubble
that surrounded us, even before our souls entwined.
Sat on the sofa at my boyfriend's flat, weed and MDMA
opening waves of conversation that only we understood.
My boyfriend sat with his own guest elsewhere.
That should have been the moment
when I embraced your efforts.
I should have paid attention to my heart then, but
typically the brain won;

luckily for me, you did not give up on me.
You did not give up on your quest for my friendship.
I did not deserve you.

I have felt your hand touch my arm
to pull me out of my sorrow.
Reminding me that the time is not yet for our reunion.
I still have things to achieve before you
come to take my hand fully.
The world was not ready for the whirlwind we caused.
It stole the wrong one away,
I shall try to not let that have been in vain.
I shall pepper the world with your memory.
I will not let them forget.
Your footsteps will manifest as my shadow,
I will take you wherever I go.

I am a vessel for the darkness;
the darkness that took you away.
I will hold aloft your torch
to burn its tendrils in revenge.
I was never a willing candidate,
now I will never be.

Tree, you are my inspiration.
You gave me hope, you believed in me,
you chose my side when no one else would.
You sacrificed your friendships with others
for your friendship with me.
I will never be as selfless and nurturing as you,
but I will always aim to be the person you believed
I could be, would be, am.
I love you, my dearest friend.
This life with your absence will be just a footnote
to the eternity we will spend together one day.

My only hope is that I still make you proud.

Intermission:
Incomplete

thirty / four / twenty twenty-one

Hey, I'm back.
Sorry it's been a while,
but, y'know, global pandemic.
So, here I am.
Sorry, no cigarette to share,
I don't smoke anymore.
Is this the first time
you've seen me addiction free?

Strange, I know.
The world has changed now.
I sometimes wonder, had you lived
would there even be a virus
stealing the world's breath;
like you stole mine, steal mine,
making it so hard to breathe
that I have to pause reality
just to exist in that moment
of empty stillness.

I may be losing the ability to hear
silence.
I didn't cry all week
just so I could do so now,
here, with you, for us;
not at home, by myself, for myself.
This is an inconvenience.
You were a tragedy.
The wound was, is, trauma.

If I close my eyes,
I can see your face complete
with its cheeky mischievous grin,

playfully content that it was
your friendship that gave me PTSD,
not the other way around, but
your eyes know what I need to ask,
say that it is okay to ask.

Can I face the trauma?
Can I move on, move beyond
without fear, without guilt?
Can we sit together now,
change my iPhone's background
from my favourite photo of us
to something just of me?
Just the lock screen though,
small steps, baby steps.

If I forgive you for leaving,
can you forgive me too?
For I finally understand that
the process of moving forward
is a process of forgetting.
Your image is in my heart,
it doesn't need to be on display.

six / five / twenty twenty-one

Please permit me one more time
to focus on one moment of past,
one tear in time that cast shadows
across centuries of silent grief.

A moment so raw and tender,
its legacy chains a future
to a ball so heavy it collides planets
like atoms creating universes of guilt.

Mountains of guilt but for what?
Cornerstones to a temple of pain.
A mourning memorial missal
written by my own hand.

You don't care, I know.
You never did beyond reaction.
My grief, my pain,
it doesn't need a public face.

these words

I sit, allow my eyes to blur vision
to tempt your ghost to jump from memory
to now, to be, to exist again, with me,
for a moment to help me just breathe.
The weight I take and just shovel aside
of words unsaid because you're not here,
and time has gone and still I'm waiting
but for what exactly I don't know...

In almost a year it will be a decade
grieving, 3650 days reliving your death,
trying to prevent and change, rewrite.
If only I could word the silent pain
of this author's pen poised above a page,
and the words I'm still unable to write.

a sacred place

This is a sacred place,
a safe place, a quiet port
in a life of storm and upset.
How dare the walk of solitude
with its mournful contemplation
be overshadowed by a darkness
created from my greatest guilt
by a sinner with the biggest lie.
A cloud who's rain so heavy
almost stopped and turned me back,
drenched in so much shame.

What monster would try to steal
the last connection between two souls
to make themselves seem godly?
Cain killed Abel for much less
and he was more worthy of memory.
Whatever shame covered me like blood,
I presented myself bare.
This is a sacred place,
there is forgiveness here.
There was always forgiveness,
it is why the connection remains.

seconds of a memory

It suffocates; so dense
a void, it is a blackhole
to emotion. Consumes all feeling.
I want to fold in on myself,
absorb these seconds of memory
and delete both from existence.
End the pain in a simple moment
like a look from hand to face.
Hand to face. Hand. To. Face.

And there I am, looking,
feeling her hand go limp, seeing—
seeing the spark extinguished.
Our universe implodes in those eyes
and I know all else is smoke.
Chasing the air to try and force
her spirit to return to her body.
Yet now I see it leave, multiplied,
each time never saying "Goodbye."

i lived

I feel like I'm a glitch
flickering between the two points.
Each image once so clear
distorting into new ugliness,
abstracting into fragments.
Thoughts, words, images of pain
collapsing in and sucking air
from lungs so tight
they fight to breathe in
fear of what they may let enter.

Not just what may get in,
more what may come out.
The voice on loop in my head
focuses the glitch to a pixel,
a black square within her pupil
and I fall into its abyss.
The void left by her absence
so universally massive,
the microcosm of my existence
passing through is but the pinprick
mine should have left in her place.

I was the one who had wanted to die.
Saved by our friendship,
by a promise we made.
My junkie heart left to beat
in tandem with hers until then
when her grip lessened,
her eyes ghosted.
The purpose of my continued existence
to be present at the ending of hers.
To be the witness to that moment.

I lived to watch my saviour die.
No.
I lived so that she did not die alone.

complet—

At that moment, the first glimpse
of the end of everything,
I breathe in the memory of completion.
Gasp in a ghostly statute to fill a void,
felt in the hollow case of my ribs.
And I hold even though everything pulls,
pulls me down into myself,
forcing another inhalation, exhalation
that removes the dream like vapour.
The tightened fist of hope opens,
fingers unfurling to reveal nothing.
The completeness she once gave lost.
Gone. Like her. Like me.

And there I am, alone
surrounded by the destruction I caused.
That child with his broken—
"What did *you* do? What have *you* done?"
Finger after finger pointed through time
to this moment to expel the life
from her body and end my happiness.
When I am good enough to complete her
the prize is death. What else would it be
when I leave only darkness in my wake?
Maybe I set her free, and one day,
when this is all done, she will return for me.

Act Two:
Twenty-Four

|

The first line, like the first glance,
always an unknown; so many abandoned,
left empty, saved from the mess I would create.
Let that one live unchallenged by my fate.
With so many side smiles I decide futures
to rest with the sighs of the past.
I have been broken and rebuilt many times,
my form so unrecognisable from birth
that what do they see now anyway?
A calcified pupa that failed to grow.

It ended with her, and started with her too.
Tied to her by a chain of trauma from
a childhood learning my place as the root
of all wrong, by a brother so badly in the—
to adults blaming me as an adult
for their wrongs, to absolve themselves.
So now, when I see her face turn to look
towards the cacophony of my monotony,
I am scared for her, and for myself.
The first glance, I know how it ends for her.
I know how it ends for me.

I know how it ends in every detail
like the lyrics to a teenage song
that has soundtracked every pain since
it struck a chord somewhere deep inside,
and echoed around a chamber that already
sat cavernously empty and unattended.
Language gave a means of communication
but it has never been about what was said.
Words are just a gateway, a key.
It's connection. Reconnection.

That's what I desire to achieve,
to reconnect to the movement of the ocean.
Reel in, raise the anchor from the depths;
free this vessel from the same repetitive tides
that have rocked and battered its sides.
Maybe there is a message hidden in here,
a cataclysm, forbidden knowledge
the waters of life have tried to shatter,
to destroy what is inside the bottle,
to save what? Continuity? Narrative?
Secrets.

So many things left unsaid, in silence,
held inside in dusty corners.
Vacant spaces like lonely eyes blink and breathe,
expand and contract, rise and fall.
A cycle of motions completed without thought.
Repetitive. Repeated patterns. Habitual.
All this I have learnt and the synchronicity of life
weaves veins of mishap beneath this skin
that channel the sorrow of childhood
to the lake that continues to fill infinite depths.
Insatiable. Voracious.

These tears are the same ones,
recycled in perpetual motion, a waterfall.
My body an Escher engine of the impossible,
regurgitating the same emotions, expelling them
unnamed, un-comprehended and raw.
An unprocessed toxic sludge that coats the skin,
hardens, and is then reabsorbed, vintaged.
A taster bottle for each year, each bitterer,
not just in taste, but in body, soul.
A full experience to explain what I cannot name,
what I choke to say.

To stand gagged, overlooking the precipice,
an illusion of calm water surfacing the pool.
Let me sit, dangle my legs above and gaze,
swallow the words behind that fist in my mouth
that I bite down on to lock the jaw from motion.
Below that film is turmoil,
crosscurrents of memories entwine and confuse;
past and past intersect, rip at each other,
form new bonds and weave tapestries that hang
like traps ready to ensnare the questioner.
Entrap. Drown in my own history.

Water is meant to be healing, healthy.
Its flow and surrender an influence to our spirits,
but this river has been dammed up,
its arteries clogged with so much silt
that the mouth has become choked.
A lake of damnation formed and stagnated;
a cesspool of self-recrimination and doubt,
fed by people who should have known better,
should have done better, but didn't
because they wanted to look better than I.
Better than the failure.

All these obstacles I have tried to face.
Blockages that although painted different
speak from the same root, a rotted core,
a charred belief branded on a child
who retreated from one world to create another.
I was a porous sponge and now I am steel wool.
In order to repair and to clean,
abrasion is required to scrape away
years of paint layered like rings of a tree;
a body of armour grown to size,
weak as tin.

I am an alloy of what I have needed to survive,
all the poisons I have inhaled, swallowed, injected.
The shards of one existence, I have crushed down,
lined up with the credit card of the next,
rolled all the receipts and sucked through a nostril.
My past paying for my future with ashes.
That first line always leading to the last
whilst habit has another ready to cut.
There is always another pipe to smoke, make,
bag of brown to tear open until you—
Stop.

Reconnect to the sound of... what?
I don't know the name for it yet,
nor the words of the language to express.
Grief is just one part, a wet part that washes,
it floods and pulls you under.
I have not drowned, although I am still
under the surface waiting.
Holding on to that final gasped breath,
trying to will myself into non-existence
to make a wish come true.

||

So I taught myself to disappear,
to hold my breath and just evacuate.
In the great universe of my consciousness
I have populated it with vast blackholes
that have devoured galaxies, ancient and in infancy.
Destructive voids that I can at will
stand upon the event horizon and watch time stop,
see those moments again and feel them pull,

draw me towards them in a way that says:
        Remember, once you lived.

What did you live for? Not 'you', I.
To seek acceptance only to run away from it?
To find love only to want more, from more?
How was I meant to understand what was good enough
when I had never been good enough?
No one took the time to know me
until she would not let me run away.
She taught me not to disappear
then turned into the biggest blackhole of all.
Now what could be good enough?

Set up at the centre of it all,
the swirling maelstrom at the heart of me.
Absorbing what came before,
monopolising all that is,
engulfing everything the future could bring.
A curious outsider transformed by her quest
through the eyes of a long forgotten child
to represent everything he desired
        – security, validation, love, a mother –
and everything that was taken away.

She came for me.
I did not seek this.
I did not seek this.
I did not seek this.
Why did she seek this?

I intrigued her, I remember she told me.
So used to everyone fawning around her,
my complete disinterest aroused her curiosity.
The icy indifference that I displayed
captivated that fire inside her.

Such opposites in nature, light and dark,
who would have thought such sought after treasure
could have been found in elements destined to extinguish.
I guess we can all be another's blackhole.

She spun herself out of alignment wilfully,
crossing a divide that widened from one side
as the inhabitants of her existence
distanced themselves for no valid reason
other than the dislike of another soul.
Someone who they had rejected,
my worth nothing but cannon fodder
when once we had all stood on the same shore.
Imagine being jealous of someone you deserted
becoming friends with someone you hence desert.

I know how she felt about all of them,
right up to that last breath;
how they spoke of me before the funeral,
portrayed themselves as golden apples
and I the rotten canker.
The great revision, did it help ease their pain?
It sure helped them walk proud and unified
as they prevented her best friend a moment.
We were all there because of me,
it would have been me she wanted to see.

And for years I've been angry at them all,
not for me, but for her. It's always about her.
Who gave them the right to forgive themselves,
to fall back on their memories and have past present as fact?
To discard her present and enforce that?
What about her memories that they turned sordid,
or didn't want to validate so just switched off?
When they gossiped and laughed about us,
where was their respect for her then?

I have been angry for her that we meant nothing to her world.

This anger is not mine to hold though.
It is rage I have held on to on her behalf.
In her name.
A physical manifestation of energy present where she is not.
I have been her fireball of disappointment.
Burning like the sun, I have watched the world move on,
the progression of people's lives, revelations,
but no one sees this hurt. I have been forgotten.
We have been forgotten like our friendship's value,
and these flames just prevent me from getting closer.

If the stepping stone is red hot,
how are we able to make the next step?

III

For the first time I just sigh on arrival.
I know there is nothing here but remains,
what connected us left ten years ago
and I attached a wish to her bones.
I have felt safe next to her physical
as it was the last place I felt safe.
To me, safety always ends in loss.
Abandonment.

There are no tears to cry today,
just a numbed acceptance. This is her grave.
It is just a grave.
The events that led to its creation
took place in a space the size of its boundaries.
Black marble marks the scene and boxes it away,
files the memory as "collected".

Processing.

I don't know what I expected to feel.
Some confirmation? Approval? Pride?
An acknowledgment for getting here, to this point?
That could never have come, not from this place;
a place of endings where I was not allowed to have one.
There is always fear here.
Always apprehension.

My grief tailored around the possible whims of others,
their reactions, comments, thoughts.
That even sat here, I am always looking over my shoulder.
Her headstone photograph tells me I need not matter,
for the first time I notice she has bags under her eyes.
"You weren't here," I tell her, and realise she was not
perfect.

IV

And then it is that day.
The cornerstone upon which all was built.
A simple morning in May that collapsed a city
and rose a necropolis in its place.
This is a grey day and I feel that way too,
monotoned, without colour across my whole being.
There seems so much more I need to say,
yet nothing new to contrast what already has.
After a decade of mourning her absence
even loss has become a memory
to be recalled and relived, fresh and familiar,
but as raw and unfiltered as the first time.
Close my eyes to breathe, close my ears to see...
I see the empty floor in that claustrophobic space,

the fist loosening its grip within my chest.

For six months I relived a moment on loop.
I saw a future implode; zero down its end of transmission.
The chaos of life reduced to a single pixel.
Blink and you could miss it. I almost missed it.
All those years spent seeking an answer,
wanting to have that closure that she requested.
How could she have left me without a word?
Created a promise that trapped me in a hell
now burdened with the weight of witness?
This moment of watching the life drain from—
That was not the moment she wanted me to see.
The memory replayed, slower. The hand squeeze.
My attention drawn from the emergency call to her,
to her eyes.
The eyes that freeze frame, hit me like a jolt,
being pulled back through time, wordless, breathless.
My body somewhere, catching up, still gasping for air.

She did say "goodbye". With that look she said it.
It was the best she could do.
The revelation seismic and changing,
just as she was a whirlwind in my life,
she continues to leave her mark in ways no one else has.
So much to unpack in what took seconds,
elongated by trauma into minutes displaced,
cut up and played out of sequence with the whole.
The intimacy of the scene expanded to grotesque.
10:46, ten years ago, I was watching her struggle with life.
10:46, this year, I am watching a coronation procession.
It seems a fitting day for change. Change and progression.
This may not be what I want, but it's what I've got.
I saw her "goodbye", I just chose not to acknowledge it.
I didn't want to accept her absence,

This is what I've learnt about complex trauma,
it keeps you locked in the past with shadows.
Shadows thrive in the dark,
to feed them, that is where you must exist.
No one can ever say that I forgot,
but I did forget myself. I became half without her.
I slowed down, I gave up. I was buried
under the weight of chains forged since birth,
clasped to my ankles in childhood,
then mercilessly added to constantly throughout a life
totally oblivious to this insanity as I thought it was care.
Unlocking the key to her was the master key.
A skeleton key that unlocked my spine,
allowing me to stand tall for the first time to say:
             That happened to me and that was not okay.

I kept her trapped in a moment so I could see her,
she hasn't died over 3650 times, I haven't lost her that either.
Just the once, and once was enough to shatter reality.
These have just been the shards of the mirror laying to rest.
Time kept her alive for a reason, to reach this point,
it needed to be now for it all to make sense.
The revelations of the past year, of this process,
root so deep it needs to be crested by her tree.
A great shadow has been banished back to its box,
its insidious control destroyed, neutralised,
the guilt it had layered burnt in a firestorm of truth.
It has to exist as part of the narrative,
but that is all it is, a plot device,
the key players are reinstated as heroes
even if no one wins in the end.

I am allowed to feel this loss, especially today,
there is no one I can share it with, nor should I.
The transfer to words weakens it and chokes in my throat.
I've suffocated on them too many times,

there's just too many to say, but never enough to satisfy.
I am allowed to feel this. I am allowed to feel.
To be aware of this fist that grips my core,
pulling me inward into myself, my own blackhole
inverting me into non-existence where I don't have to feel,
where I never had to feel, never had to see her leave.
I am allowed to close my eyes and wish for ghosts,
hold my breath in shallow flutters, curling my toes,
because ghosts are all I have left
now that the nightmare's laid to rest.

Maybe when I get to the end and pen the final word,
it won't be a tale of loss, but of love.

V

When I speak of endings
I speak, too, of a totality,
a complete passing. *La fin.*
The ultimate conclusion to all of this.
There had always been hope,
a tiny spark that on my fortieth
she would just reappear at my door,
the tickets to New York in hand as planned.
Life could just go on and all this could—

Everything is now all past.
There exists no future in our friendship.
No impossible events that I can hold her to,
no promises she can break by her absence,
no expectations from me, no more waiting to see.
She could never have just walked back in,

the justification of all that pain could not be ignored.
Another lump in the throat, a pulled in stomach,
I don't know what to write,
because I still don't want to let her go.

Not completely, but no one should expect me to.
I just don't want to give up on that dream I had
although I'm aware of its impossibility and magnitude,
and how everyone has been proven right, again.
"There's stupid Dom, believing in fairy tales."
That little boy who cried when he left Primary School.
"What are you crying for? So stupid."
I'm sorry, mum, but endings feel like empty train platforms,
so used to watching things go.

And here I am again,
the train leaving in slow motion.

I'm running, trying to catch one final glimpse through a window.
Another part of my life being let go and all I can see
is the reflection of who I now am.
When she died, I denied myself the luxury of closeness.
Her place remained filled as I could not do it again,
I could not betray her memory or my sanity
welcoming in the prospect of future calamities.
From the platform's end I wave to it now.

I have held myself ransom by so many phrases;
so many repeated accusations that waterboard my conscience.
Tortured myself with a four word sentence looped infinitely:
      I wasn't good enough
for her, to save her, to prevent the events from happening,
for not being able to turn back time and just die in her place.
Always apologising to a memory for not being something I was,
never once considering the alternative,
that she could say to me: "Sorry, I wasn't good enough."

I hear those words and I'm back to my birthday,
lying in bed daring her to break that final promise,
to prove once and for all she is fallible,
that all promises get broken, just like all fairy tales lie,
but again, it's not about her, she is just the effigy.
What is being challenged is the normality of a reality
impressed upon a defenceless child
where disappointment and insecurity are king.
For once things had been different.
Now they are just the same.

Yet they weren't, once more they had changed,
that final passing had released us from each other.
Unbound by mortal words, time was allowed to move forward,
a great sigh as the second-hand swung forward,
all others following as a new hour chimed.
Nothing can ever be the same again.
Not because of her, but because of her.
The insight salvaged from the embers of her death
has allowed me to feel closer to her in that moment,
when it mattered, when she was all that mattered.

A decade of reliving, of cycling around the same guilt,
believing the same insecurities, and challenging
words that she, herself, had said as truth
to people that actually held worth to her,
can now be laid to rest in some way.
I have cried so many tears over those years
and now when they come they empty me momentarily.
The reservoir drains and I feel spent.
I feel that moment pass in a way that I can finally say:
     I have grieved.

VI

Now is your time of grief. *[John 16:22]*
A time to learn a new language,
a new rhythm of words, a new vocabulary.
A visceral and tactile library that connects
physical experience to emotional depth,
inner biology to the external world.
Leave the world of shadows and spectres,
meanings and sequence;
embrace the undefinable nature of existence
and the raw brutality of life.

Everything has been brought back down to size.
A photograph that exploded outwards from its frame,
shattering glass across a void in slow motion,
an ever expanding universe of crystal fragments
that were nothing but reflections of the original
has been gathered up, as best they can,
and poured into the blackhole at the centre
where the photograph use to be.
It's still there, on the horizon. Trapped
in time, in its past.

As a child I was never that fascinated by space.
The wonders of the solar system rarely interested me.
My dreams were never on that scale.
I dreamt of death and tragedy,
daydreamed of being orphaned.
Imagined myself escaping into so many alternatives
that the pain of their non-existent past
ate away at the core of the present
as I saw versions of myself I could have been
if only—

If only what? That poor child;
with her help I have scratched the surface,
a new understanding with myself that had been lost,
huddled in some dark space in the void inside me,
and now I can see him, I don't know what to say.
I know I'm as guilty in part as those who created him
for keeping him shut away and silenced.
But I am what he created to survive,
I am the product of the very silence he languished,
don't I have the right to be angry?

There it is again, that word:
Anger.
It's the one emotion I have been trying to find,
the one that across a decade has been quick to burst
at the mention of her name, her death, our friendship.
Yet here, at the end, there is nothing but a flatline.
I want to feel it, I want its spark to ignite embers,
relight the inferno inside so I can feel and understand;
not all these new connections to the tangible parts of me,
my throat is a dry lump and I wish it was for her,
but I know it is for an unanswered question about myself.

I am exactly where she hoped I would be,
in a place where I would be learning more about me,
finding my hidden depths without a need for others.
Independence, acceptance, forgiveness,
I bestow these all upon myself.
No one experienced what she and I did.
We were the only witness,
only I have the right to how that is remembered,
that is, as it is, was:
a final moment between best friends.

Moments are all we have, and all I can have,
from the guilt of moments missed, moments can be found

in phone conversations at wasted locations
whilst wasted highs were spent with wasted connections
I wish had died instead of her.
Physicality is not important, she was everything in-between.
I chose to let her in during a moment on a staircase in a club,
covering me so I could take a bump of speed.
I imprisoned her on a staircase in my flat,
forgetting that the only blackhole in our friendship was her ass.

Release the funny memories, unlock the vault,
share her to people, make her live through me.
I have kept her to myself for so long,
so scared to lose her again to the world
that I have denied her from myself.
There doesn't have to be a conclusion,
she can be with me every time I mention her name,
every time I think about her, or look at a photograph of her face.
She can be with me for as long as I want her to be.
No one can take that away.

I cannot change one part of it,
for no matter how an element has changed,
its presence in the narrative of our journey remains intact,
to remove it would be to erase a phrase from our story,
nothing would make sense.
Everything in my life led to that point,
destined or otherwise, there could only be that point;
and now I have been led to this one,
visually the very same, that point2,
multiplied by my past, and now divided by the present.

Do I finally have an answer?
Could I ever? I mean, truly?
I can never pull my eyes away from the screen;
this is one piece of newsreel that I'll never not rewatch,
trying to find some justification.

I'll just never know, as I'm not meant to,
it isn't for me to have that knowledge.
Just as that child will never know why
an adult accused him of causing the same death
those decades prior.

Life is a cycle, we don't need to create our own.
I think back to the cathedral in France,
shouting at Christ, not in anger,
but in tiredness. Tired of the same old shit repeating.
Constantly, on loop, in new disguises.
That is the word I've needed throughout:
     Tired.
I'm tired of repeating, of being stuck in this past,
watching people move on whilst I hold a memory as tribute.
I watched myself step into shadow
and sadly saw that nobody around me cared.

I was in the shadow with the only one who did,
both our hopes and dreams were dead.

If I sit and let myself go there, it's instant.
I'm back on the stairs, she's next to me,
I'm on the phone to the emergency services,
her hand squeezes mine and I look,
I see—
I saw the end, I saw the life leave her body,
she fell back in slow motion as though deflating,
words spilling out of my mouth,
something seismic occurring in the space of a grave
because that's where it ends.

I know it ends, and now the memory isn't as intense.
It is just a replay of an event.
The sequence has found its way into its place in the past,
sits there uncomfortably, but secure. Over.

There is nothing more I can do.
I watch as an observer, as I should be.
I've played my role in that scene, it's been filmed;
no matter how many times I've called for retakes,
the production is over, new films have been made,
the leading lady died.

So now I stand staring at the corpse of her,
I know where this falls in the memory,
after I've been taken to the police station,
when she's experiencing death to herself for the first time alone,
so this is new. A continuation.
She is stood next to me, staring down at herself.
"Well," she says, "that wasn't meant to happen."
"You're telling me," I reply.
We stand in silence and I know this is goodbye.
"At least I died without wrinkles."

AFTERWORD

This is a collection I wish I never had to write. The twenty-three poems that make up the first Act were written in 2019, in the weeks, days, leading up to the anniversary of my friend Tree's death, when instead of turning to my usual vices to manage my grief, I turned to poetry. Tried for the first time to get my thoughts about her death out of my head and into the world.

When Tree died, I was part-way through my first course of therapy – *Mentalisation-Based Therapy for Borderline Personality Disorder* – and she was the only one of my friends who actively showed any support. At the time, she was meant to go travelling, and we made plans that we would meet up with each other in Peru to celebrate the new "Dom" I would be at the end of the treatment. That never happened. In my head, she still went travelling, and never came back.

2023, ten years after her death, I was in the final stage of my latest course of therapy – *EMDR for C-PTSD.* Every week, I had to relive the final moments of her life; after a decade of tears, in those sessions I released the combined emotion tenfold. Now part of the therapy was to move the traumatic image forward, to create a different ending. That is what the final Act of this collection is, why it has its title. It was written, once again, in the weeks, days, leading up to the tenth anniversary of her death. My journey through therapy had started with her by my side, hoping for a bright new future, and now, it ended with her. Full circle.

I held on to a ghost for a decade, as I believed she was the only person who truly believed in me, because she was the only one who had the courage to show it. The essence I should have held onto was myself, that was what first attracted Tree to me, what she wanted to emerge, and what has a future. Ghosts belong to the past, it is the memories that keep the person alive.